Sleeping with Rivers

For Gail
and
Mimi

Cath Drake
Sleeping with Rivers

Winner of the
Mslexia Poetry Pamphlet
Competition, 2013

Poetry Book Society
Pamphlet Recommendation

SEREN

Seren is the book imprint of
Poetry Wales Press Ltd
Nolton Street, Bridgend, Wales

www.serenbooks.com
facebook.com/SerenBooks
Twitter: @SerenBooks

ISBN 978-1-78172-184-1
Epub 978-1-85411-186-5
Mobi 978-1-78172-185-8

A CIP record for this title is available from the British Library

The publisher works with the financial assistance
of the Welsh Books Council

Cover image by Barbara Madden
Author photo by Naomi Woddis

Printed by 4edge Ltd, Hockley

Contents

7   Sleeping With Rivers
8   Serious Sleep
9   The River People
10 Finding Australia
11 The Man With No Heart
12 House of Bricks
13 The Beginning of Youth
14 Cartoon Boy
15 Mr Jacob Never Seemed To Have Much
          Backbone
16 The Dove
17 The Drake
19 Sunken Garden
20 Interchange
21 Rope Fragment, River Walk
22 Out of the Study
23 Octopus
24 It Didn't Happen Until University
25 The Circle Line
27 The Whole World Might as Well Know
28 The Queensland Box Tree

30 *Acknowledgements*

Sleeping with Rivers

Every morning she wakes up with rivers
and their capillaries cut across her face.

Yet her pillow is down, its cover brushed cotton
and she's tried orthopaedic beds.

Her father says she sleeps hard,
that the force of her sleep creates currents

across her cheeks, that she craves the suction
of sleep drawing her towards the earth

like a stone thrown down a well. She says
she travels in her sleep: first rivers, then oceans,

deserts, snow-crusted mountains, forest canopies,
along muted seabeds and the linings of clouds.

She speaks with plovers and godwits
on their pilgrimage of thousands of miles,

the electric tentacled siphonophores and
the once-thought extinct fanged-frog inside a crater.

In the mirror she traces their furrows
and as they fade she feels young and plain again.

It won't be long, her father tells her, before
you wish every morning was as pink as the last.

Serious Sleep

The earth has tipped as I fall,
caught in the gravitational pull
of the great safe ship of my bed.

I tunnel toward the centre
as I hear a timbered voice say:
there's no other way, sweetcakes,

follow the blue trail. I try to wake
but I'm scooped deeper, flailing
in blurred versions of future and past.

The dense core is too black,
too sharp to recall. And when
the Gods of Sleep finally let me go,

I float to the surface, waking
in sub-levels first: my too long legs
tucked in a ten year old's bed,

at a wooden school desk,
a holiday house by the Indian Ocean,
then my rose duvet is there

and sliding into focus a wardrobe,
a door, a window, the sky outside
in full swing, my beached body.

I test one thought at a time
and stretch toward the wide-angled
world that has shifted on its axis.

The River People

One day they just arrived, camped for days
on Heirisson Island, waiting for swans,
but none came. We don't know who they were,
why nobody moved them on. They were sun-blushed,
ethereal, used hand signals we'd never seen before.

On our daily commute across the highway
from island to city and back, we watched
their canvas tents and sometimes a figure or two
of a man, woman or child walking in the hot dust
like a mirage. The bridge's heavy traffic drowned

any sound of the birds, tides, their daily doings.
Then they asked us when the swans disappeared.
Would you notice if a highway, a skyscraper,
or if the river vanished and there was just gravel
under your feet? Would you still call this place

Swan River? We felt their heavy ochre eyes.
They made a swan shrine from a mass of grass,
bark and reeds: its beak pointing skyward,
long pampas grass feathers flying in the breeze.
Every time we crossed the bridge we felt the loss,

imagined their reflections in the water swimming
with the glossy black swans, and then one day
they just went. We didn't get to ask them anything.
The shrine eventually let go into the wind,
blowing into the river, into our Swan River.

Finding Australia

(for Miss Brockman)

We learned the directions of the compass, names of brave sailors
who sounded like philosophers, coloured in their sailing ships,
drew map after map that tracked noblemen spun by wild winds
who tried to find spices, and almost found Australia.

Unwieldy ships were washed up on far-flung reefs or islands.
When finally they found it, they put up flags on hilltops, nailed
plaques to trees. Captain Stirling was certain he'd found Perth,
so certain he brought boatloads of people down the Swan River

to witness it, commission paintings, build houses, forge roads.
Australia was young and proud, our future was on a plate.
We filled our project books with drawings of early settlers
in smart soldier outfits, women in long skirts and bonnets.

They kept on finding as they trekked through rugged terrain
to discover more and more of what had not yet been found.
We coloured in more maps, listened to stories of hardship
when tattered men perished for us in search of an inland sea.

Then our eccentric year nine social studies teacher whispered:
Terra nullius? terra nullius? Australia was not discovered:
there were already people here right across the beaches,
plains, forests and deserts, who knew every bump and echo.

She showed us slides of black men in chain gangs, eyes disjointed
with shock, frightened black women in shift dresses, archives
of river poisonings and battles for land where only one side won.
She showed us modern photos of black people on reserves

with scattered rubbish and makeshift houses staring out of the dust,
told of a whole generation of children taken from their parents.
There weren't any pictures of brave men in sailing ships.
I wondered if we'd dreamt it all and what else they lied about.

The Man With No Heart

He's a loner it's true but you'd barely know
he's different except the way his T-shirt pulses
around the dip in his chest, and how he stares

at our fighting and falling in love.
Sometimes you see him on the street
watch a couple embrace or a lost child crying.

He'd put a hand to the hole sensing it throb
like a man who's lost a leg still feels it move.
When he was born they had to cut out his heart:

it had rotted in the womb like bad fruit.
You'd think he'd always cover it up
but sometimes he stands out in a field,

eyes closed, shirt off, letting the breeze
blow right through; his veins around the wound
ballooning like a frog might breathe, testing

the strength of his skin against the force of air.
He knows we're looking, enjoys our curiosity,
our envy. Head aloft, he sings: *this is who I am*.

We wonder how our rag-and-bone hearts
keep going. Each time we lose someone, it helps
to think of him and the cool breeze in the field.

House of Bricks

They say a house of bricks can stand up to a wolf
with breath like a hurricane. My dad grew up
in the Depression: he knows. In our house of bricks,

there was no Depression, but I dreamt of a hurricane
that levelled our house. I could see the wolf panting
next to the rubble, very pleased with itself

while we huddled in torn pyjamas; my sister
cradled her doll that had lost a leg and whispered
don't worry, over and over into its plastic ears.

My parents pretended to make soup in the ruins.
When I woke up I went round the house pressing
walls and floors, the heavy dining table,

but when I sat in the big chair in the lounge
I could hear the wind howling down the chimney –
the beast warning us. My parents made a hearty roast

in our house of bricks and that's what counted.
Never speaking about the child who died
would not matter in a house as strong as this.

The Beginning of Youth

When I was young I breathed shamelessly,
Catching dust and butterflies on my tongue.
I dug into the sky with dirty fingernails
And curdled the earth with feet dragged in mud.
When I was young, I chased stars as they fell
And lay on the ground with them as they fizzed out.
I swore dog blunt and cackled crow mad at clouds.
I tiptoed in long grass, collecting polished stones,
Raising quartz to my eyes and straining to see through it.
I told off supermarkets, bus stops, people in bleached houses,
Watched my fingertips unpeel, nails drop off in a trail of blood.
I picked up lost things like separated playing cards,
Bottle tops, broken pencils, four-legged stars.
I made nests from blankets and toys with a red-nosed dog
At the helm who barked 'keep out'.
I squeezed a real dog so hard it squealed
And took off a knuckle of my flesh.
I passed round the iron and singed blurred lines across my body.
I combed my electric hair and unfurled my arms,
Showing their soft insides and they said it was unsightly.
Then I brought up the earth in several choking heaves.

Cartoon Boy

My brother was a cartoon fiend. He liked chase 'em ones best:
Roadrunner, Scooby Doo, Transformers, Inspector Gadget.
They'd bend universal laws like plasticine: walk through walls,
take impossible dives into waterfalls, pass the moon on the way.

He'd sit in his pyjamas with his soggy rice bubbles next to him
on the big-armed velour lounge. With his eyes closed
he'd guess what was going on with all the squeaking and crashing
junkyard sounds of falling, catching, running away, saving!

Then he'd think of something in the kitchen or shed that made
those sounds: scissors, toaster, drill, rattling saucepans,
eggs cracking, water running down a clogged plughole, his voice
like the excitable horns and cymbals in cartoon crescendos.

At the closing credits, he'd say: *we could do all this, me and you.*
He was charmed by the slap of pancakes and Mum was smug-sure
she could hand over the cooking soon. Dad was proud of his son
dedicating hours to hammering and grinding. He smiled to himself

that my brother would be a fine carpenter, our houses full
of baroque furniture. I revelled in the beauty of all their dreams
and imagined my brother's face peering out of a huge scrapyard
as he fine-tuned with the tiniest screwdriver you've ever seen.

Mr Jacob Never Seemed
To Have Much Backbone

He never stood for much. Never sponsored
a student on a walk-a-thon. Nothing
stirred him. If you asked him a question,
he wouldn't give a straight answer.

He'd blubber something so we had no idea
what he meant. We wondered how his maths students
would have coped if it wasn't for text books.
No-one knew how long he'd been around:

his suit the colour of the soupy carpet.
At staff meetings, he'd look gluggy, his face
translucent, eyes submerged. You wouldn't hear
his rubbery limbs when he came up behind you:

his weightlessness, his tap on the shoulder
like a surprising sponge. His office grew dank
with over watered plants, five water jugs –
it wasn't a casual interest in the fish tank.

Miss Green caught him trying to climb into it:
an arm submerged, face dripping. His giddy stare
frightened the English teachers, while science teachers
explained: *rocks, pinned insects, test tubes,*

we all have our obsessions. This was different.
And it was a mistake to send Mr Jacob
on the Year Nine seaside trip. He just gazed
at the sea. He was useless with the students,

then halfway through the beach cricket game
a kid threw seaweed at him. He seemed to like it,
took it in both hands, stood up, walked
like a man in a trance into the water.

Miss Green called out to him to no avail.
He never came up for air. No-one went after him.
They didn't find a body, just a huge jellyfish
washed up in the bay and his useless glasses.

The Dove

Yellow sun-rings around its eyes, pleats of faultless
feathers, wise wrinkled claws – it tipped its beak
toward the wood where the sky takes over

in folds of air, the landlocked world sinking
smaller and smaller. I glanced away and the dove
was gone without a sound or flash of wing tip

so perhaps it had powers even lighter than flight.
I spent all day in the shed: white paint everywhere,
dribbling down my arms, into shoes, enamelling fingertips.

Later I emerged trussed in my white dressing gown
with my wooden-veined tissue paper wings
strapped to my back. I could barely walk like this –

struggled up the back door steps and lifted my arms,
heavy with intention like the hollow roar
of a wave before it breaks. My wings fanned open,

my world lit up, became kingdom-sized. But I couldn't leave
the ground with my clodding feet, just stood transfixed,
dissolving into some far-off star and that dove's stare.

The Drake

Now that I think about it, there was always a swampy smell.
Often a smudge of mud across the kitchen tiles:
I'd examine the shoe rack but all the soles were clean.
I thought all backyards had leaves, twigs, gumnuts, snails,

and many feathers even though we were miles from a lake.
A neighbour asked me once: do you have a chicken?
At times, I'd wake in the night to what sounded like a horn,
but then silence, no engine. These things happen in a city.

After the silence there was a scuttling that could've been
any wide flat feet slapping on concrete paving.
The first time I saw him it was an ordinary day:
he stood there in the yard on an upturned pot plant,

his blue-green-fawn sculpted feathers like a painting.
I carried on with my homework, didn't think that much of it.
But I know it was the same drake that turned up at school:
at first perched on the windowsill, preening, then

under the desk next to me, so when I went to read out
my project to the class, its honk made me stutter
and I slipped on his damp trail. In assembly they asked
who wanted to join the choir, but I didn't get up –

he was jammed between my ankles and I didn't want
to tread on his flippers or cause a stir from his shrieking.
He'd follow me home and it took me much longer to ride a bike
because of his flapping about. Maybe he did mean well

but I wished he wasn't there when I plucked up the courage
to talk to Sean Chambers. He kept ducking under my feet
so I walked funny and that day he smelt really badly of pond.
I kept my distance from Sean in case he thought the whiff was me.

At high school, I took up table tennis: it was good for balance,
timing and duck dodging. We even won a knock-out tournament,
the duck and I: despite his struts across the table,
his spluttering at the umpire. When I got the trophy home,

he watched as I inscribed 'the drake' under my name in ballpoint.
I daydream of one day strolling past a lake when I'm old
and see him, looking me in the eye, standing just like he did
on that flowerpot with his perfect feathers, watching me go by.

Sunken Garden

When I hear talk about the Sunken Garden that would appear
suddenly behind gum trees along the track beside the lecture theatre,

that stage framed by rough limestone, the lemon-honey wattles,
peppermint trees, fresh-cut grass on a cool sleeveless night –

it reminds me how we'd go there after wine and cheese nights, half-cut,
talking Mead, Sartre, Barthes and how easily those years slipped.

One night, when the drink suddenly hit you, you could barely walk,
sinking into the damp ground. How much we cried on the stone seats

and couldn't articulate what for. When I think of that place and you
in that gorgeous jade fifties frock you got for a bargain at an op shop,

your warm brown limbs flailing about, I wish I could have slowed it
to a second by second frame, stepped back: told you just how much

you had to offer, to stop wasting time, I'd always goddamn back you.
Even the blue-cloaked moon, watching coolly, loved you.

The sprinklers came on without warning, making us run to the bus;
we called out and waved goodbye across opposite sides of the street.

Was there something I could have offered that night when you
were trying to grip with both hands and things were starting to slip?

Interchange

I see him, well-dressed, carrying a buckled briefcase
over the other side of the train track at the station;
he's going to the sea and me to the mountains.
He's in his twenties with slicked black hair,
a slim strong body, a fixed gaze. He'll spend time
in the top floor of an end terrace, fish for his dinner
and it'll eventually become his business.
His loneliness will be important to him, the breeze
off the water in winter sometimes enough
to know he could have been a different man.

But no, still he's there, over the other side of the tracks,
an old man wishing the sea, wishing back forty years
and though his heart isn't good and his cough rattles,
he knows he could gut a hundred silvers of fish in a sitting.
His briefcase is full of black sand and a mash-up
of love and leaking roofs, pride and cold tables.
He paces the platform in damp furrowed boots
while I stare out from a mountain window
as the heavy buzz of insects draws down the days
and the moon shines silver across the valleys.

Rope Fragment, River Walk

Was it a slashing storm that came spiralling
    from unearthly pressures high in the clouds
        that burnt right through the rope cleanly

or a slow gnawing, the boat long abandoned,
    left to fill with water, wrestle with the jetty,
        tug desperately before loosening and drifting?

I see a smiling man raising two glasses, beckoning me
    to trust the step from solid ground to the constantly
        moving boat. We float out to the river mouth,

lulled by midday warmth, clinking our glasses.
    I say: *It's so still, I can see the sky in the river.*
        Then as the sun cools and the current gets stronger,

I hook an arm through his and we take the jut of waves
    together. He says: *what do you think about in the dark?*
        Then cups my head to rest on his shoulder.

Cut long ago, the rest of the rope is somewhere intact,
    coiling away, drifting, buried deep in the river
        or swept further out, swirling on the seabed.

Out of the Study

I emerge covered in froth and seaweed, awash with words
      as if I've floated out too far.
Streets look watermarked, people and shops appear on rafts
      in an endless blue.
Those people talk in fishbowls while I gather their musings
      into some far-off land,
then notice my handbag makes a sharp clip as I open it
      and suddenly I'm back
two centuries ago strolling the common across the road
      in a sweeping long dress,
lace-beaded bodice to the neck, boots knitted to the ankle.
      The bemused shop keeper repeats:
That's two-twenty, thank you. I'm surprised
      how much a few pieces of fruit cost nowadays
and wander back home thinking I really should
      garden or clean for a while.

Octopus

Underwater, I watch
him climb through the gnarled jut
of reef and muddle of seaweeds.

He doesn't see me
as separate from the sway
of water. Surprised

he does not fight
and how liquid soft he is.
Tentacles curl around an arm;

a shudder from spine
to toes stops my breath
for a loaded moment

while his breath,
that subterranean blur
of wind on water, takes over,

merges with my skin.
I'm not afraid of swollen head,
goggle eyes, ink.

I hold still,
lift him out of the water.
He flinches to adjust

to dry air. I hear
a camera shutter on the beach
as he fumbles

over my rough swimsuit
back to the suck of skin,
slides onto my thighs,

fingers for the water
and then is gone.
I still dive for him.

It Didn't Happen Until University

I said I'd done everything else: just not that.
My room-mate, Sylvia, was astonished.
She lit a candle and said: *tonight it'll burn down.*

I could already smell his musty wood polish skin,
hear his late night arguments on existentialism,
his heavy feet shuffle while I'd try to sleep.

I turned up late and unannounced. He smiled
like he knew everything. I never said I wanted love,
just to know what the thing was, to be one of those

who could be fresh picked. He stroked the curve
of my lace vest, saying: *very nice, very nice.*
He said he was falling in love with me, but I knew

he fell in love often. I was in love with longing
and thought only of flesh, leaving the rest behind.
It was a strange thing to be doing with two bodies,

especially in the awkward moments, the urgency
paused, legs stuck together, everything exposed,
the birthmark on my thigh lit red. Wrapped in a sheet,

hair dishevelled, I was surprised when I saw
my dewy face in the still white of the sink.
That was the best part: I remembered I was blessed

with the enamel skin of gods, perfect brown limbs.
Afterwards, we sat back to back as if we'd not yet
learnt to speak face to face. *Sex is sex,* he said,

as though I had simply joined the human race.
We argued. The tea was tepid. When I got home
Sylvia said: *I told you, I told you,* while I cried.

The Circle Line

He says he saw me first at Kings Cross dashing
down the stairs, straight onto the train, loosening
my purple scarf, my chequered overcoat, panting
with relief, but I say it was Moorgate, when I noticed

his long black coat with its upturned collar appear
in my carriage as he intently studied a tube map,
pretending not to notice much else, as you do,
and although he says it had nothing to do with

the crowd thinning out at Monument, I'm sure
that's when he started to look up that bit longer,
loosening his lips as he saw me glance back,
incidentally, he said I sideways-smiled at him

at Cannon Street, but I must have been daydreaming
since I don't remember that particular stop at all
and it wasn't until Mansion House that I realised
his gaze had an intensity the exhausted tube crowd

didn't have as he picked up his paper, pretended
to read, then put it across his knee and sneaked
a look at me after a long intake of breath, repeating
this several times, and I also took out my book

and did the same, then at Temple our eyes coincided
and we stared at each other, my pulse ticking,
and at Embankment he daringly asked me:
what are you reading? when he could see

the cover from there and I answered just the title
of the book as though I was giving him my full name
and number; he pressed his mouth shyly as if
I'd told him much more and I think he suspected

I'd planned to get off at Westminster or maybe
St James Park and walk back but I felt heavy in my seat
and stayed and when he stood up at Victoria, an obvious
place to change, I shifted uneasily on my seat,

but he was only stretching his legs, then lost his seat,
moved one closer, asked: *is it a good book?* then
opened his paper, I opened my book, he uncrossed
and crossed his legs, several times, as did I,

then at High Street Kensington I rummaged my bag
for a tissue I didn't really need and started to muse
on why anyone would take the Circle Line all the way
round rather than cut through on the Central Line

and at Paddington, I wondered if anyone would notice
if I passed the stop where I got on as I watched him
diligently clock each station as we went by,
shuffling nervously, but at Baker Street, he sighed,

nodded, held my gaze with lowered eyes for at least
two full seconds as if to acknowledge that a chance
to make a dash south on the Bakerloo or Jubilee Line
and beyond was completely, expertly ignored

and I nodded back, pleased, as Baker Street felt like
an important mark of commitment and as we kept
circling, each time we pulled into Baker Street
there was a half smile or a raised eyebrow, but

neither of us was sure where the beginning or end was –
after several Baker Streets we exchanged a bold sentence
or two and it felt almost disappointing and inevitable
that at some point we would have to disembark, somehow.

The Whole World Might as Well Know

I'm not supposed to tell you this, but I love
    the way your hip-slung jeans tense
around the buttocks, how fine-spun skin flares
    from delicate neck bones, long legs end
in perfectly-tuned ankles and the violet light
    in your almond eyes. I shouldn't say this
but I love the way you spin tales: espionage,
    confessions. You cup the fluidity of things,
split life open through the gut and live there,
    thriving on tropical fevers. When you turn over
stones you always find something shining, alive.
    I'm in love today. I want to take you out
for salmon bake, slow wine, a rush of flaming
    chocolate liqueur sipped with you.
Sweet reflection, swing past that shop window
    again, I love the way you do that!

The Queensland Box Tree

This is my world, where I let my sandals drop
onto the grass below amongst the swaying pussy-tails,
the dandelions looking up at me like sun-winks.

This sweep of lawn, this forested garden in front of me,
the hedge leading to the letterbox, this house,
the street, these lowlands – this is my kingdom.

As I climb higher, the road trails off the edge
of my world: rooftops, tiny people carrying bags.
The top branch bows under my weight,

but it knows me well enough to hold.
The creamy flowers around me smell as sweet
as oranges and peaches. I balance on one foot

and when I slip, I catch with both arms –
hug a wooden limb, press it against my cheek.
Arms and legs scratched and alive, mouth full of spittle.

My magnetic sun, my vastness, my burning days,
my place etched on the landscape, rooted
and always lifting, lifting, holding.

Aknowledgements

I acknowledge the following publications which previously published versions of these poems. 'Octopus' was published in *Indigo 4* (Tactile Books, Western Australia, 2009). 'It Didn't Happen Until University' was published in *Rialto* (2010). 'Sleeping with Rivers' was published in *Westerly* (University of Western Australia, 2012). 'The Whole World Might as Well Know' and 'The Man with No Heart' were published in *Bliss* (Templar Poetry, 2011). 'The Man with No Heart' was also published in *Not Only the Dark* (Wordaid, 2011). 'The Queensland Box Tree' and 'Mr Jacob Never Seemed to Have Much Backbone' were published in the *Loose Muse Anthology Volume 1*, (2012) and 'Interchange' was published in *Loose Muse Anthology Volume 3* (2013). 'House of Bricks' and 'Cartoon Boy' were published in *Southbank Poetry* (2012). 'Serious Sleep' was published by *Axon Journal* (Canberra, Australia, 2013). 'Finding Australia' was published in *In Protest: 150 Poems for Human Rights* (2013, published by The Human Rights Consortium, University of London). 'Sunken Garden' was published in *Brittle Star* (2012).

A huge thank you in particular to the Arts Council England for support in completing this manuscript and to my wise and invaluable mentor Mimi Khalvati. Many thanks also to Amy Wack and the staff at Seren.

Heartfelt thanks to many fellow poets who have helped me, including Malika Booker, Roger Robinson, Jacob Sam-La Rose, Jacqueline Saphra and Malika's Kitchen members who encouraged me so generously when I started to write. Thanks to so many inspiring teachers and poetry friends along the way, including Moniza Alvi, Roddy Lumsden, Pascale Petit, John Hegley, Jocelyn Page, Saradha Soobrayen, Baden Prince, plus my talented Poetry School seminar group, Advanced Poetry Workshop group, my monthly group (Kate, Alison, Kayo, Peter and Nicola) and members of The Vineyard. Also thanks to many supportive friends in the UK and Australia who always give me warm encouragement including Eva, Gail, Kathy, Eitan and Margo.

Thank you to the generosity of Barbara Madden for allowing me to reproduce her photograph on the cover and to Naomi Woddis http://www.naomiwoddis.com/ for the portrait photo.

Poems written in the first person that refer to family members don't necessarily reflect my real family members.

The Author

An Australian living in London, Cath Drake has been published in anthologies and literary magazines in UK, Australia and US. She has performed in many cafes, bookshops, theatres, festivals and for unsuspecting passers by. She runs writing workshops to recharge creativity and is passionate about taking poetry and creative writing to new spaces. In 2012, she was short-listed for the Venture Poetry Award, awarded an Arts Council England grant and was writer in residence at the Albany Arts Centre café. She is also a copywriter and non-fiction writer and her work includes award-winning journalism, writing for radio, oral history and life stories. http://cathdrake.com/